WOMEN'S
BASKETBALL

GOODYEAR
Physical Activities Series

Edited by J. Tillman Hall

Archery	Jean A. Barrett *California State College* *at Fullerton*
Badminton	James Poole *Tulane University*
Bowling	Norman E. Showers *Southern Illinois University*
Fencing	Nancy L. Curry *Southwest Missouri State College*
Folk Dance	J. Tillman Hall *University of Southern California*
Golf	Edward F. Chui *University of Hawaii*
Men's Basketball	Richard H. Perry *University of Southern California*
Soccer	John Callaghan *University of Southern California*
Social Dance	John G. Youmans *Temple University*
Swimming	Donald L. Gambril *California State College* *at Long Beach*
Tennis	Barry C. Pelton *University of Houston*

Fundamentals of Physical Education	J. Tillman Hall *University of Southern California* Kenneth C. Lersten *University of Southern California* Merril J. Melnick *University of Southern California* Talmage W. Morash *San Fernando Valley State College* Richard H. Perry *University of Southern California* Robert A. Pestolesi *California State College at Long Beach* Burton Seidler *California State College at Los Angeles*
Women's Basketball	Ann Stutts *San Fernando Valley State College*
Women's Gymnastics	Mary L. Schreiber *California State College at Los Angeles*

FORTHCOMING BOOKS

Handball	Rollin Wright *University of Illinois*
Men's Gymnastics	Gordon Maddux *California State College at Los Angeles*
Volleyball	Charles "Randy" Sandefur *California State College at Long Beach*

 GOODYEAR PUBLISHING COMPANY
Pacific Palisades, California 90272

Goodyear Physical Activities Series

J. Tillman Hall: *Series Editor*

Ann Stutts

San Fernando Valley State College

WOMEN'S BASKETBALL

WOMEN'S
BASKETBALL

Ann Stutts

Library of Congress Catalog Card Number: 69-17997

Current printing (last number):
10 9 8 7 6 5 4 3 2 1

Printed in the United States of America

Acknowledgments

I wish to express my deepest appreciation to Jerome Noss for the photographs, and to Anita Aguilar for typing the manuscript.

Editor's note

The Goodyear Publishing Company presents a series of physical education books written by instructors expert in their respective fields.

These books on major sports are intended as supplementary material for the instructor and to aid the student in the understanding and mastery of the sport of his choice. Each book covers its fundamentals—the beginning techniques, rules and customs, equipment and terms—and gives to the reader the spirit of the sport.

Each author of this series brings to the reader the knowledge and skill he has acquired over many years of teaching and coaching. We sincerely hope that these books will prove invaluable to the college student or any student of the sport.

In WOMEN'S BASKETBALL, Ann Stutts discusses basketball history, giving a vivid picture of how society, at the turn of the century, viewed girls who "dared" to play the game.

The book presents to the student the various skills and concepts needed to play and understand the game. Ann Stutts further describes in detail offensive and defensive maneuvers. Many court diagrams show the positioning of the players during the various plays. The young ladies who demonstrate the individual basketball techniques have a very healthy look—contrary to the dire predictions of the 1890's.

Whether you are a coach, player, or spectator, you will find that WOMEN'S BASKETBALL will give you a greater understanding of the fundamental concepts, strategy, skills and techniques of this fascinating game.

Contents

Key to Diagrams

O   OFFENSIVE PLAYER

X   DEFENSIVE PLAYER

⟶   PATH OF PLAYER

----⟶   PATH OF BALL

〜〜⟶   DRIBBLE

⟶| SCREEN

WOMEN'S BASKETBALL

Historical Background

Women's basketball is a contest between two opposing teams of six players each. The original game as conceived by Dr. James Naismith in 1891 was governed by 13 simple rules and was developed in order to occupy young men's time between football and baseball seasons. Within weeks of the first contest, however, a group of college women were involved with a woman's version of the sport.

Few techniques or strategies were used in the early days. Present techniques and strategies have developed as a result of an involvement in basketball by countless people over the years. Perhaps Dr. Naismith would have difficulty recognizing the present game. There is no doubt, however, that the objective of the game then and now remains the same—namely, to put the ball into the basket. The team able to accomplish this most often during the allotted time is declared the winner of the contest.

The modern basket is a metal ring 18" in diameter, attached to a backboard. Usually a bottomless net is attached to the metal ring. Calling this contraption a basket is a carryover from the original version of the game when two peach baskets were nailed to the sides of a balcony. The game was played for several years before anyone thought of cutting the bottom out of the goal so that the ball would drop back down to the playing court. And because there was no longer any need for someone to climb up and retrieve the ball the game's pace was greatly increased. Constant change and modification of the rules have been, and continue to be, the way of basketball. In the many years of conflict concerning rule changes and modifications it seems ironic that the basket remains 10' high above the playing court simply because that was the height at which those original peach baskets were nailed to a balcony so long ago.

Many valuable experiences are inherent in the game of basketball. Each participant reacts to it in different degrees and intensities. These experiences have physiological, sociological, and psychological value for the player. The following comments and observations are taken from various periodicals in which women's basketball was a topic of consideration as early as 1896. An article entitled, "Basket-Ball at Smith College" appeared in *Outlook*[1] magazine in that year. "Basket-Ball for Young Women," in *Harper's Bazaar*,[2] appeared four years later, and in 1902 an article entitled, "College Girls and Basket-Ball" was written for *Harper's Weekly*.[3] The following excerpts from the article in the latter indicate the social climate for women's basketball of that time.

> In the gymnasiums of the majority of colleges and schools, basket-ball is one of the principal methods of pastime and exercise.
> The college girl who goes in for athletics is just as much in earnest as her big brother, but she goes about the matter in a different way. The boy is proud of his

[1]"Basket-Ball at Smith College," *Outlook*, Vol. 54 (September 26, 1896), pp. 557-58.

[2]J. P. Paret, "Basket-Ball for Young Women," *Harper's Bazaar*, Vol. 33 (October 20, 1900), pp. 1563-67.

[3]"College Girls and Basket-Ball," *Harper's Weekly*, Vol. 46, (February 22, 1902), pp. 234-5.

athletic inclinations and ability and fond of displaying his prowess to an admiring public. His sister may be no less conscious of her skill and strength, but it is not good form to court notoriety, and thus it is that we hear much less of the girl athlete. Nevertheless, in college circles and among the girl's intimates, her reputation as a star player is as well known and discussed as are the feats of her sturdier relative.

Basket-ball is a favorite with college athletic instructors for the reason that it furnishes at one and the same time a fascinating pleasure and the finest scope for all-around exercise. It is work and play combined. The good points of the game are being more generally recognized and it is fast acquiring a popularity that promises to place it among the leading college sports, not only among the girls, but in the boys' colleges as well.

At Smith College basket-ball leads all other athletic diversions by a large margin. When a Smith girl becomes a good basket-ball player, she at once acquired athletic and social prominence in her college circles. To make the Sophomore or Freshman team is a distinction that she strives earnestly for. In so large a school as Smith, and where there are so many candidates, this is no easy matter, and there are long days of hard exercise and faithful training . . . . While there is no training-table and she is allowed full liberty as regards her food, she is, nevertheless, expected to abstain from candy, sweetmeats, or other things that might prove a detriment to her strength and wind. As the time for the spring games approaches she is very particular about her hours, and invitations to late social events are politely but firmly refused. To a girl this means as much as or more than it does to a young man, and it may truthfully be said that, in a way, the young woman is a martyr to her athletic ambition.

Twenty-five years later, in 1928, an article in *Hygeia*[4] expressed objections to participation in basketball by girls, especially in the interschool game. The article gave the

[4]H. S. Curtis, "Should Girls Play Interschool Basket-Ball?" *Hygeia*, Vol. 6 (November, 1928), pp. 607-8.

following reasons for these objections in terms of social considerations: Women have not been trained for interschool competition and lack the traditions of sportsmanship impressed upon men's teams for generations. Women are poor losers and often lose their tempers. Women are more unstable than men and as a result of the games they cannot adequately handle their studies, lose sleep, and suffer general nervous injuries.

Several reasons considered the physical aspects in support of these objections: A woman's heart is smaller than a man's and therefore not well qualified to handle the strain of playing basketball. Bodily injuries are likely to be more serious for girls than for boys, especially those which occur while jumping or falling. These sometimes result in a displacement that could require an operation to prevent sterility.

The motivation to participate, as well as the benefit derived from basketball, varies from individual to individual. Some people play basketball because they have to do so as part of a required class. Others are motivated to participate in order to derive the biophysical values of the activity. Still others participate because they want to *move*, to "play basketball." One can view the playing of basketball as a nonverbal form of human expression achieved through the medium of human movement. Just as the musician may express herself in terms of music as she plays her instrument, and the artist by manipulation of brush and paints, so the basketball player expresses herself through the technique and strength of careful body movement.

Fundamentals

Good basketball is based on the ability to perform the various fundamental skills properly. Some of the most commonly used fundamental skills essential to game play are discussed below.

BODY CONTROL

Proper body control in basketball requires the ability to move within a confined space with other players and to avoid contact with them. It is necessary to start, stop, run, pivot, jump, and change direction quickly while maintaining complete body balance.

Body balance is the basis of the execution of individual basketball skills. Perfect body balance is necessary to permit the player to move quickly in any direction. To achieve this type of balance, the knees are slightly flexed and the weight is evenly distributed over both feet and supported toward the balls of the feet. The feet are spread about shoulder width apart, or wider, depending upon the position of the body. The lower the body weight is carried, the wider the feet should be spread. There is a slight forward bend at the waist

5

with the back in a straight but comfortable position. The head is held up to provide for proper vision of the court situation. The position of the arms is determined by the offensive or defensive responsibilities of the player and will be discussed in more detail in a later chapter.

The ability to move quickly the moment the situation presents itself is an important requirement. Therefore, to start quickly lower the hips, flex the knees, place the feet in a stride position, and push forcefully from the feet with the body in a forward stride position. To *change direction* smoothly shorten the stride in one direction while lowering the weight and pushing with one foot as you take a full stride in a new direction.

There are two methods of stopping in basketball. In both methods the weight is lowered from the hips and the distance between the feet is widened. The head must remain over and centered between the feet for maximum balance. One method is the *stride stop*, which is executed by planting the forward foot firmly and stepping through with the back foot. The second method is the *jump stop*. It is accomplished by controlling the weight with a slight jump that permits both feet to contact the floor simultaneously. The jump is very slight; it is not a hurdle motion. The weight must be lowered over the heels to prevent further forward motion.

The *pivot* is a maneuver that allows the player with or without the ball to change direction. The player with the ball is allowed to turn in any direction as long as one foot remains in contact with the court. This foot is referred to as the pivot foot.

Figure 2.1   Change of direction.

The rules state that once the pivot foot is determined it cannot be changed. When the player comes to a two-step stride stop, only the rear foot may be used as the pivot foot. Either foot may be used as the pivot foot after a jump stop when both feet have contacted the court simultaneously, and after a one-step stop. When catching the ball while standing still, either foot may be used as the pivot foot.

Figure 2.2   Jump stop.

Figure 2.3   Pivot foot.

Player catches ball

Pivot foot→

2nd step

TWO-STEP STOP
Rear foot
must be used
as pivot foot

Player catches ball

ONE-STEP STOP
Either foot
may serve as
pivot foot

Player catches ball

Feet touch floor simultaneously

JUMP STOP
Either foot may serve
as pivot foot

The pivot may be executed with either a forward or backward motion around the pivot foot. In either case it is important to keep the weight low and on the ball of the pivot foot throughout the movement. Figure 2.4 shows a backward, or rear turn.

HOLDING THE BALL

The first concern of a player with the ball is to hold it properly. The ball is "gripped" by the fingers and thumbs, not the palms. The hands are placed toward the sides of the ball with fingers spread comfortably apart.

Figure 2.4   Rear turn.

Figure 2.5   Holding the ball.

RECEIVING AND PASSING THE BALL

A player must be able to catch the ball before she can consider passing it. When receiving the ball the hands are relaxed with the fingers spread. Upon contact with the ball the hands and arms give in the direction of the approaching ball to absorb the force of the pass. The player should watch the ball all the way into her hands. It is a good idea to form a habit of carrying the hands above the waist while playing on offense.

The *chest pass* is one of the most common types of basketball passes. The ball is held at chest height in both hands with the elbows comfortably close to the body. The fingers are spread around the side and the thumbs are behind the ball. To deliver the ball take one step forward and at the same time extend the arms with a flick of the wrist at the end of the extension. The palms should finish facing down and to the sides. This pass is directed toward the chest area of the receiver. The range of this pass is limited to the player's ability to pass the ball to the receiver in a line of flight parallel with the floor.

The *bounce pass* can be used in a crowded situation to bypass the defensive players. This pass is made with the same general type of action as the chest pass. It is directed toward the floor at a spot about two-thirds of the distance to the receiver.

Figure 2.6   Chest pass.

The ball rebounding from the floor should reach the receiver between the knees and waist. If the ball is bounced too close to the receiver, it will be difficult to handle; if it is bounced too far away, it will be slower and easier to intercept.

The *two-hand overhead* pass is used to get the ball over the defensive player. It has become increasingly popular and is extremely effective against a zone defense if executed properly. The ball is held over the head in both hands with the elbows slightly flexed. It is delivered with a forward motion of the arms and snap of the wrists. Avoid dropping the ball behind the head before delivery. This pass should be received about head high.

Some general points to remember when passing are:

1. Work toward making the pass with as little windup as possible.
2. Try to "snap" or "flick" the pass with the wrists and hands. The beginner may find it necessary to step forward in the direction of the pass.
3. Avoid slow, long, looping passes.
4. Use fakes to conceal your intended action and try not to telegraph the pass.

Figure 2.7 Two-hand overhead pass.

5. Pass to the side of the receiver away from the defender.
6. When the receiver is moving, pass in front of her or lead her with the pass.
7. Reduce the speed of the pass when the receiver is moving toward you.

SHOOTING

One of the most important fundamentals of basketball is shooting. There is not a player on a basketball team who is not required to shoot at some time during the game. If no one is able to put the ball into the basket, then the effects of the other fundamentals are rendered relatively useless. The following are some of the most common types of shots.

The *layup* is the easiest shot in basketball. It is a high-percentage shot, made close to the basket, using the backboard as the point of aim. This shot is executed after receiving a pass while moving toward the basket or at the end of a dribble toward the basket.

The beginning right-handed player approaches the basket at an angle of about 45° to the basket from the right side of the court. Later the shot should be practiced from both sides and at all angles to the basket. As the player catches the ball from the pass or dribble a step is taken first with the right foot, then with the left. As she steps on her left foot, the right knee is raised forcefully in the upward jump toward the basket. At the same time the ball is taken up over the head with both hands. As the player approaches the maximum height of the jump the left hand is taken away and the right hand gently lays the ball against the backboard. Aim for a spot that will allow the ball to rebound into the basket. This spot will vary with different combinations of players, ball, angle of shot, and backboard. The left arm is held approximately at shoulder height for added protection from the defensive player. Remember to allow for the speed at which the approach is made and gently lay the ball against the backboard. The player should learn to take the layup shot with either hand.

The *jump shot* is one of the most effective shots in basketball today and the most difficult to defend. Generally, women find it hard to execute this shot because it requires strength in the arms and wrists. The following is a functional progression of shots to gradually develop the jump shot.

The *one-handed set shot* is the first shot in the progression. The ball is rested on the nonshooting hand and is "gripped" by the fingers of the shooting hand, but does not rest on the palms. The fingers of the shooting hand are spread and placed slightly to the side of the ball rather than directly behind it. The wrist is cocked. The elbow is in close to the body. The hand is in line with the elbow, and the shoulders are squared to the basket. The foot on the side of the shooting hand is placed forward. The toe of the rear foot is about even with the heel of the forward foot, with the feet a comfortable distance apart. The knees are slightly bent. The aim is sighted over the top of the ball. There are varying opinions regarding the point of aim. Some aim at the front part of the rim, some just over the rim, and others consider the basket as a whole target. Regardless of the point of aim selected—remember to watch the target.

The shot is executed by an upward push from both feet in a coordinated extension through to the arm, with a final

Figure 2.8 Layup shot.

forward snap of the wrist. The ball is pushed from the fingers and rolls off the middle and forefinger last, resulting in a natural backspin on the ball. During the follow-through the feet may leave the floor slightly.

Learn to execute the shot within a few feet of the basket and gradually increase the distance. The distance from which the shot is practiced must never be such that it will create a change in the basic form described; however, the player must allow for the necessary adjustment to increase force. The finger force is for fine control.

When the player has developed this shot from as far back as the free throw line, she can use it when taking her free throws. For this only one shot pattern had to be learned.

When the player can shoot a one-hand set consistently from the distance of the free throw line, the next step in the progression is the *one-hand overhead shot.* Everything remains the same as in the set shot with the exception that the ball is raised over the head with the wrist laid farther back and the aim is sighted from under the ball and through the forearms. Once again practice is started within a few feet of the basket.

Finally, the *jump shot* is a one-hand overhead shot with a jump added. The ball is released when the shooter is in the air at the maximum height of her jump. It is necessary to learn the shot jumping straight up and coming straight down to avoid

Figure 2.9 One-hand set shot: Starting position and just after release.

contacting the defensive player on the follow-through. Caution should be taken to avoid drifting to the sides.

The difficult part of the shot is the timing for the release of the ball. If the ball is released while the player is still going up, there will be a tendency for the shot to be long, and if the ball is released while on the way down, there will be a tendency for the shot to be short. Remember the ball is released at the height of the jump.

The following rules apply for all of the shots described:

1. The player should strive for vertical body movement during the shot, with very little forward motion.
2. The shot is a total body action with full extension from the feet through the wrist to the finger tips.
3. Control the shot with the fingers to develop a soft "touch" on the ball.
4. The range of a particular shot depends upon the individual. The area of the court within which a player can consistently shoot using correct techniques is her individual shot range. This may vary from within 10' to beyond 20' from the basket.

Figure 2.10 Starting position one-hand overhead shot.

Figure 2.11 Jump shot.

DRIBBLE

The dribble is a skill that permits one player to control and move the ball around the court. Some of the most common uses of the dribble are to move the ball into the offensive area of the court, to drive toward the basket for a layup, to move the ball out of a congested area of the court, and to move into position for a shot. There are many other times when the dribble can be used effectively; however, it can be the most abused skill in basketball. So remember: Do not dribble when a pass would be more effective. Dribble only with a definite purpose in mind.

While dribbling, the ball is controlled by using the forearm, wrist, and fingers. The fingers are comfortably spread. The ball is pushed, not "slapped" or "batted" to the floor. As the ball rebounds from the floor the fingers meet the ball and move up with it a few inches before pushing it back to the floor.

Learn to dribble without looking at the ball. This permits the player to view and remain a part of the total court action. Learn to dribble equally well with either hand.

A *control dribble* is used to move the ball when defensive players are near. The body is in a crouched position with the

Figure 2.12   Finger action during dribble.

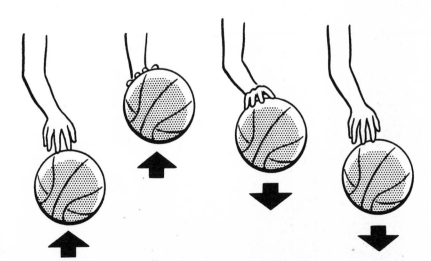

elbow close to the body. The ball is bounced slightly to the side of the body and should rebound about knee high.

The *speed dribble* is used when the player is not closely contested by the defensive players. The body is in an upright, running position and the ball is bounced to the side of the body. The ball is pushed forward and rebounds higher; for this reason the dribbler is able to move faster across the court.

REBOUNDING

Rebounding is the technique used to gain control of the ball after an unsuccessful attempt to score. It is generally considered, all things being equal, that the team which controls the majority of the rebounds wins the game.

When rebounding, the player attempts to jump up and toward the ball. The timing of the jump should permit the player to gain control of the ball with both hands while at the top of her jump (see Fig. 2.15). As the player returns to the court the ball is quickly pulled into position about chest high

Figure 2.13   Control dribble.

with the elbows out and legs spread. This position helps the
player protect the ball from her opponents (see Fig. 2.16).

It will be necessary to practice rebounding frequently so that
the angle and force of the ball rebounding from the backboard
can be studied. These factors are important in developing the
anticipation essential to the proper timing of the rebound.

Figure 2.14   Speed dribble.

Figure 2.15   Controlling the
rebound.

Figure 2.16   Protecting
the rebound.

Individual Offensive Techniques

After the player has become skillful in passing, dribbling, and shooting, she is ready to consider the individual offensive maneuvers that will permit her to effectively perform these fundamentals in a game situation.

OFFENSIVE STANCE

The stance necessary to execute the offensive maneuvers is basic to all aspects of the game. The knees are bent and the body is in a slightly crouched position. The head is up, permitting vision of the basket and other players. The foot corresponding with the shooting hand is advanced. The ball is held close to the body in both hands. From this stance the player is ready to shoot, dribble, or pass.

PROTECTING THE BALL

Several maneuvers are used to protect the ball from an opponent. While looking for an opportunity to dribble, pass, or shoot keep the ball moving and try to avoid extending it away from the body with the arms. Instead, keep the ball close to the body with the elbows out and move the ball by rotation of the wrist and hands. At times the player has to use her body to help protect the ball. This is accomplished with a pivot, but a player should avoid turning her back to the basket or major field of play, especially when she is near the sideline or endline.

DRIBBLE

The dribble is a necessary offensive maneuver. To move the ball effectively with the dribble, a player must be able to use either hand to protect the ball from her opponents and to change its direction. When the dribbler is challenging the defender, a controlled dribble is used and the ball is maneuvered in the space between the dribbler and her guard. However, when the defender is pressuring the dribbler, a technique to protect the ball must be used. In this situation the body of the dribbler is kept between the opponent and the ball. To increase this distance, the free arm can be flexed and raised to the side of the body.

A change of direction can be accomplished in two ways depending upon the position of the defensive player. The quickest way is with a change of hands in front of the body.

Figure 3.2   Protecting the dribble.

Figure 3.1   Offensive
stance—player ready to
pass, dribble, or shoot.

When dribbling with the right hand, step with the right foot and at the same time place the hand slightly to the side of the ball and push it diagonally across the body. As a step is taken with the left foot in a new direction the left hand receives the ball and continues to dribble.

When more protection is needed, the player must keep her body between the opponent and the ball throughout the move. To do this when dribbling with the right hand, the player steps forward with the left foot and pivots on it, then swings the right foot back and around. The ball is changed to the left hand as the pivot is being made.

FAKES

A player must be able to maneuver for a shot when the defense plays her closely. To accomplish this, *fakes* are used. Fakes can be made with the eyes, head, shoulder, feet, ball, or with any combination thereof. The dribble and pivot are combined with these fakes to outmaneuver the defense. The maneuvers, often called moves, do not come naturally but must be learned. The following move will serve as a basis to develop this ability.

The *rocker step* is a move designed to produce a drive. Using either foot as the pivot foot, the player takes a half stride with the free foot in a forward or sideward direction, faking in

Figure 3.3   Change-of-direction dribble.

that direction with the head or shoulder. It may be necessary to return to the start and repeat the action until the defensive player reacts to the movement. If the defender does not fully commit herself to the fake, the offensive player pauses briefly and pushes hard from the pivot foot and drives for the basket in that direction.

If the defensive player follows the initial move of the rocker step, the offensive player recovers and within the same move initiates a *cross-over step*, pushing hard from the pivot foot and making her drive on the opposite side of the defensive player.

In either case the first step is the important one. The length of the stride will vary with different players and situations, but keep in mind the larger the stride, the slower the step; the shorter the stride, the quicker the step. The player must try to outmaneuver her opponent with the first stride. The dribble is executed with the outside hand. The ball is released low and pushed as far in the direction of the basket as possible but still kept under control.

The offensive player should also learn to fake a shot and then drive or fake a drive and then shoot; thus she becomes a double offensive threat. For the *fake shot and drive* the player trains her eyes on the basket and starts bringing the ball up for her regular shot. She brings it right up to the release position without giving away her ultimate purpose. When the defensive player commits herself to the fake, the offensive player drives

Figure 3.4   Rocker step.

past. The secret of the move is the ability to go from an upright position into a low driving position quickly. Remember to keep the ball low on the dribble.

OFFENSIVE MOVES WITHOUT THE BALL

When the offensive player must free herself from the defensive player in order to receive the ball, she can accomplish this by varying her speed, by changing direction, or by stopping and pivoting. Often a combination of these movements is required.

The offensive player has two different objectives when working to receive the ball. One objective is to receive a pass while closely guarded. The simplest move used to accomplish this is for the player to take a few quick steps in the direction away from the ball and toward the basket. Then she suddenly reverses direction and moves toward the ball. This strategem not only gives her an advantage over the defensive player but also frees her to receive the pass.

The other objective is to cut or break toward the basket and to receive a pass for a possible layup shot. The rocker step and cross-over step are effective moves for this purpose. It is easier to receive the pass if the offensive player cuts between her opponent and the ball; however, it can be accomplished with a cut to either side.

Figure 3.5   Cross-over step.

ONE-ON-ONE SITUATION

A one-on-one situation designates the maneuvers of one offensive player against one defensive player. The first responsibility of the offensive player in this situation is to analyze her opponent. If the defense is playing loose, shoot from the outside. If the defense is playing tight and the offensive player is without the ball, cut behind the defense and look for a pass from a teammate. If the defense is playing tight and the offensive player has the ball, she should be prepared to drive. Watch the feet of the defensive player and try to take advantage of any mistake she might make. For example, she might cross her feet or stand up straight. If the defensive player is in a forward stride position, it is usually wise to drive to the side of the advanced foot.

Ability to perform effectively in a one-on-one situation requires many hours of practice. The success of a team effort in both offense and defense depends upon the players' abilities in the one-on-one situation. The individual offensive techniques covered in this chapter will serve as a basis in this situation. The next chapter will cover the defensive aspects.

Figure 3.6   Fake shot and drive.

Individual
Defensive
Techniques

The success of a team's defense depends upon the player's ability to execute the individual defensive fundamentals. Regardless of the type of team defense employed the individual defense will remain basically the same.

BASIC TECHNIQUES

The defensive player's *stance* must allow her to move quickly in any direction as she reacts to the moves of the offensive player. The knees are bent and the hips are lowered. The weight is evenly distributed toward the balls of the feet. The feet are about shoulder width apart, or wider, with one foot in advance of the other. The upper body is bent slightly forward at the waist; the back is straight but comfortable, and the head is help up. Usually one hand is held close to the side to discourage the pass. The hand position varies with the position of the ball.

To provide for maximum mobility and quickness the *footwork* of the defensive player is built around a sliding step. The feet are never crossed unless the player has lost her defensive position and must run to regain it. This movement transfers the weight by taking a small, quick slide with the foot closest to the desired direction of movement. The opposite foot glides toward the lead foot.

In a forward stride position the leg nearest the closest sideline or baseline is in back. When the offensive movement is toward the rear leg (open side of the stance), the first movement is with the back foot and the advanced foot follows.

Movement toward the side of the advanced foot (closed side of the stance) requires a slightly different reaction to avoid losing the advantage of a position ahead of the dribbler. The first move is a short, quick step with the rear foot as the advanced foot moves to the rear foot position.

FLOOR POSITION

The most important aspect of individual defense is position. The primary rule is *stay between the player and the basket* or in special situations between the player and the ball. If the defensive player is forced within a few feet of the basket, the first rule is useless. The player must establish and maintain proper position—she should not just "chase the ball."

Figure 4.2 Guarding the shooter.

Figure 4.1 Individual defensive stance—front hand points ball.

DEFENDING THE PLAYER WITH THE BALL

Even though there is a set of general rules, many variables must be considered when defending the player with the ball; namely, the combination of size, quickness, shooting and ball-handling ability.

When the offensive player has the options of driving, shooting, or passing, you must take precautions to prevent all three options in the order listed.

As the ball is brought into a shooting position raise the hand that corresponds with the advanced foot. Move the hand between her eyes and the basket. Continue to keep the knees bent and the weight low. Do not jump, lunge, lean, or try to steal the ball. If your opponent has not dribbled, leave enough distance between you and the offensive player to prevent the drive. As a rule maintain a distance of at least an arm's length from the opponent. React to all fakes with a quick step backward. Another measure to help prevent the drive is to adjust a half body position to the opponent's strong side. For example, if she can only drive effectively to her right, overplay her in that direction one half of a body width in relation to her feet.

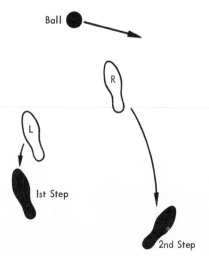

Figure 4.4 Defensive footwork—movement toward side of advanced foot.

Figure 4.3 Defensive footwork—movement toward side of rear foot.

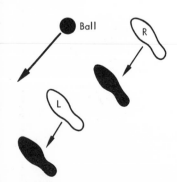

The primary responsibility of the defensive player is to maintain proper position between the opponent and the basket—it is not to try to steal the ball. As the offensive player starts to dribble attempt to maintain an advanced or "fronting" position in the direction of the dribble. One half-step to one step ahead of the player, or an arm's length, is the proper distance. If the defensive player follows the offensive player in a "trailing" position, she must either foul or allow the drive as the dribbler approaches the basket.

When trying to deflect the ball away from the dribbler use the hand corresponding with the advanced foot and flick upward from the floor aiming at the bottom of the ball as it rebounds from the floor. Two of the most common mistakes when defending the dribbler are: (1) trying to steal the ball, and (2) losing a "fronting" position and extending the arm, knee—or both—in trying to compensate for the mistake.

Figure 4.5 Defensive adjustment —overplay half body width.

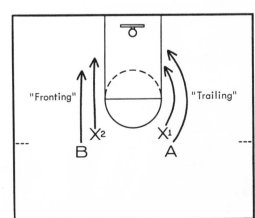

Figure 4.6 Fronting and trailing defensive paths.

At the completion of the dribble the defensive player moves in closer trying to force the offensive player to turn her back to the basket so that she cannot attempt a shot. When the offensive player does attempt a shot, the defensive player must "block out" the shooter trying to get the rebound. To accomplish this the defensive player turns toward the basket and blocks her opponent's first move to the basket. She then tries to gain possession of the rebound.

DEFENDING THE PLAYER WITHOUT THE BALL

After the offensive player passes the ball she becomes a possible cutter. At the release of the offensive pass, the defensive player should quickly retreat several steps back and slightly in the direction of the pass. One hand points toward the ball, the other at the passer. Do not relax or straighten up, and try to maintain vision on both the ball and your opponent. If it is impossible to do both, maintain vision on the offensive player without the ball.

Try to prevent the player without the ball from receiving it in a position advantageous to her. Drop back toward the basket and try to anticipate the moves of your opponent. Do not

Figure 4.7 Blocking out the shooter.

merely trail her around the court. A player who cannot get the ball cannot score. Often it is advisable to pressure the pass from the rover to a forward, trying to force the forward to move up high to get the ball and thus force her to move from the area of the court where she is most effective. In this situation the defensive player very aggressively overplays the forward. She keeps the foot that is closest to the ball forward, and her corresponding hand up and in the passing lane ready to deflect the pass. She must maintain vision between her player and the ball and make it as difficult as possible for the forward to release herself for the the pass.

ONE-ON-ONE SITUATION

We have seen that the offensive player must analyze her opponent and play her accordingly. The same holds true for the defensive player. Determine from where and how effectively she can shoot. If her outside shooting is weak, you may want to play her loose, thereby giving her the outside area of the court. Determine if the opponent can move equally well to the right and left. Often a player will have a favorite move or will only be able to drive to the right or left. Overplay her strong side, thereby forcing her to move to her weak side. Determine her ball-handling ability. If she is a weak ball-handler, try to

Figure 4.8 Pressuring the pass receiver.

pressure her into making a mistake. Finally, but certainly not last, determine her speed. If she is slower than you are, play her very aggressively; if she is faster than you are, you will have to increase the space from which you guard her, or play her loosely.

Below we have summarized some of the important individual defensive points that you should keep in mind:

1. Keep between your opponent and the basket or between her and the ball when she is near the basket.
2. Point the ball with the front hand.
3. Maintain a "fronting position" or stay ahead of the dribbler.
4. Never cross your feet, except when you have lost your position and must run to catch up with the offensive player.
5. Study your opponent and try to anticipate her moves.
6. Never lunge at the ball or reach in with the hand to make up for a poor defensive position.
7. Attempt to dominate your opponent; be aggressive.
8. Keep your knees flexed and weight low in good body balance. Do not be caught standing straight up and unprepared to move.
9. Never jump to block a shot or leave the floor until after your opponent has jumped.
10. When a shot is taken, block your opponent out for the rebound.
11. If your opponent gets past you, run as fast as possible and try to re-establish your position.
12. Don't give up. The spirit you bring to the play is no less important than the basic techniques you develop.

TERMINOLOGY

BACKBOARD   The surface to which the basket is attached.

BACKCOURT   That half of the court which contains a team's defensive basket.

BACKDOOR   A term to describe the direction of a player's cut; it is to the side of the defensive player, away from the ball.

BLOCKING OUT   The defensive maneuver of positioning to prevent the offense from getting the rebound.

CLEAR OR CLEAROUT   An offensive maneuver to move the defense out of an area, thereby creating space for an offensive move.

CONTROL GAME   An offensive style with slow, controlled movements designed to take the percentage shot.

CONTROLLING THE BOARDS   Obtaining the greatest number of rebounds.

CUT   A quick offensive move to gain an advantage over the defense, ideally toward the basket. Also referred to as a break.

DEFENSE   The players who try to prevent their opponents from scoring.

DOUBLE TEAM   Two defensive players guarding the player with the ball.

DRIVE   A quick dribbling move toward the basket.

FAKE   A body or ball movement designed to deceive an opponent.

FAST BREAK   An attempt to move the ball into the offensive half of the court quickly, thereby outnumbering the defense and gaining an offensive advantage.

FREE LANCE   An unstructured type of offense where players take advantage of whatever offensive opportunities arise.

FREE THROW   An unguarded shot for a goal as the result of a foul by the opponents. Also referred to as a foul shot.

HOOK PASS   A one-handed circular pass over the head.

HOOK SHOT   A circular one-handed over-the-head shot.

OFFENSIVE REBOUND   Obtaining a rebound on a team's offensive end of the court.

ONE-ON-ONE   The situation where one offensive player tries to score against one defensive player.

OUTLET PASS   A pass made after a defensive rebound, usually toward the closest sideline of the court.

OVERLOADING   Having more than one offensive player in the same defensive area of a zone.

PASS AND CUT   A pass to a teammate and a cut toward the basket for a return pass; also called a give and go.

PLAYER-TO-PLAYER   A team defense where each player is responsible for one particular offensive player. Also referred to as man-to-man.

POST PLAYER   A player who moves around the lane area, and often plays with her back to the basket. Also called a pivot player.

PRESS   A forcing pressure defense in which the offense is challenged at half court, three-quarter court, or full court.

SAGGING DEFENSE   When the defensive players who are away from the ball drop back and crowd the lane area.

SCREEN   A maneuver by a player to legally position her body to the defense in such a way that she will temporarily free a teammate for a drive or shot. Sometimes called a pick (block).

SCREEN AND ROLL   An offensive maneuver where the screener cuts toward the basket as the defensive switch is made. Sometimes called a block and roll.

STALL   An offensive maneuver to control the ball while making little effort to score. It is usually used late in the game to run out the remaining playing time.

SWITCH   A defensive maneuver to change guarding responsibilities in an attempt to combat a screen.

THREE-ON-TWO   A situation in which the defense is outnumbered three to two, usually seen at the end of a fast break.

TURNOVER   Loss of ball possession without there having been an attempt to shoot at the basket.

Forming the Offense and Defense

To form is to make something into a definite shape or pattern. In basketball six individuals are formed into a team by establishing certain patterns of cooperative movements.

OFFENSIVE COMBINATIONS

There are four offensive players in women's basketball. These players are classified according to their beginning positions on the offensive court. Two players are called forwards and two are called rovers. The forwards play several feet out from the endline and free throw lane with one forward on either side of the basket. The rovers play near the top of the free throw circle, one on either side.

The passing opportunities, or passing lanes, are limited because of the presence of the four defensive players between the offensive players and the basket. The safest passing lanes are limited to the teammates immediately to the sides of the player with the ball, but not across the lane from her. A pass from a rover to rover, rover to forward, or forward to rover on the same side of the court is possible. Passing from forward to forward is not advised.

The established offensive patterns follow certain rules. The beginning rule is that the player with the ball is to initiate the play action. An offensive player has three options, or choices: She can shoot, pass, or dribble. If the player can find a shot in a one-on-one situation, nothing more is needed. A cooperative effort with a teammate is necessary to allow for a one-on-one or to assist in making shooting opportunities available. This assistance is an unselfish team effort and is one of the most satisfying experiences of the game.

When the shot option is prevented by the defense, the player may choose to pass the ball. To initiate a play pattern she can either:

1. pass and cut to the basket
2. pass and move toward the ball and screen
3. pass and screen away from the ball
4. pass and hold position

TWO-PLAYER PATTERNS

A *pass and cut* is a two-player pattern initiated by a pass and followed with a cut to the basket. It can be made in one of two directions. In one pattern, the cut is made directly to the basket; in the other, the move is made around the outside of the receiver and then to the basket. Another name for a pass and cut is *give and go*.

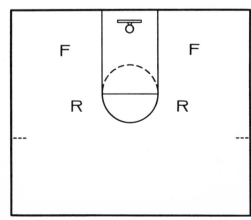

Figure 5.1   Offensive court positions.

In the cut directly to the basket the player with the ball passes to a teammate, fakes in one direction, and cuts toward the basket in another direction trying to lose her defensive player and to clear herself for a return pass and shot.

If the cut is made between the defensive player and the ball, the return pass can be made easier than when the cut is made to the opposite side of the defensive player or backdoor. The backdoor cut should be made when the defensive player is overplaying or turns her head to watch the ball.

The second option is for the player to pass and cut outside the ball. When space is available, the passer may break around the outside of the receiver who hands the ball off to the passer as she cuts close by. This frees the cutter for a possible drive to

Figure 5.2 Pass and cut to basket. Player A passes to B, cuts toward the basket, and receives a return pass from B.

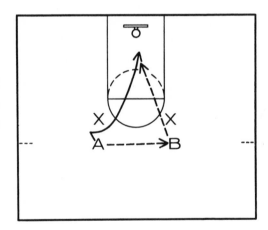

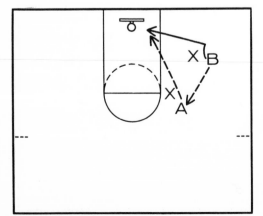

Figure 5.3 Pass and cut backdoor. Player B passes to A and cuts backdoor; B receives a return pass from A.

the basket. This pattern works best from the rover to forward position.

Another option on the outside move is for the passer to stop behind the receiver who hands her the ball. The position of the receiver will screen and free the passer for a possible shot. The position between the two players should be about an arm's length, allowing sufficient space to attempt the shot, yet it should not be enough space for a defensive player to block the shot.

The second type of two-player pattern is a *pass and screen*. In this situation the player passes the ball and moves toward it. This move usually involves some type of screening action. The screen is a maneuver by a player to position herself on the court in such a way that she frees her teammate momentarily of a

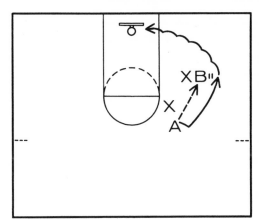

Figure 5.4 Pass and cut outside—drive. Player A passes to B and cuts to the outside of B. B hands the ball off to A who drives to the basket.

Figure 5.5 Pass and cut outside—shot. Player A passes to B and cuts to the outside of B for a return pass and possible shot from behind B.

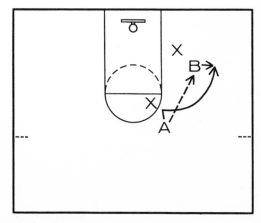

defensive player. The screen may be executed as either a moving or stationary maneuver. When a moving screen is used, caution should be taken to avoid contact with the defensive players. When a stationary screen is used, the screening player should not extend her arms to the side or move into the defensive player. After she has served her purpose as the screen, she rolls toward the basket. Usually the stationary screen patterns are preferred over a moving screen pattern.

The following is a two-player screening pattern when the screen is set laterally as in a rover-to-rover or rover-to-forward pattern. For example, Rover 1 passes to Rover 2 and moves to set a screen on the defensive player guarding the player with the ball. The screener will establish a position close to the side of the defender with one of her feet on either side of the defensive player's closest foot.

The rover who received the pass must wait until the screen is set to avoid pulling the screener into a foul or allowing the defensive player to slip over or behind the screen. The distance between the defensive player and the ball must be within an

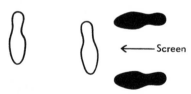

Figure 5.6   Foot position for lateral screen.

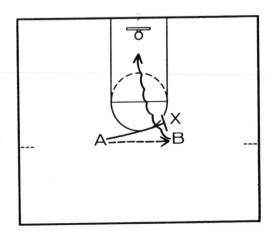

Figure 5.7 Pass and screen—drive option. Player A passes to B and sets a screen for B. B drives to the basket.

arm's length to make the screen effective. If the distance is too great, the defensive player will have room to slide over the screen and move with the dribbler. It is the responsibility of the player with the ball to force this adjustment. Timing is crucial. Once the screen is set, Rover 2 dribbles around her teammate's screen freeing herself for a possible layup or percentage shot near the basket.

If the defensive players change or switch opponents to prevent the drive, a second option is available. This option involves a roll. The roll is a move made by Rover 1 as the defensive players switch to cover the drive (see Fig. 5.8). As the dribbler starts to move the screener pivots, opens up in the direction of the drive, and cuts for the basket. As the defensive players are switching the pass is made to the screener who is rolling. This move requires precise timing with a teammate (see Fig. 5.9).

Figure 5.9 Pass and screen—roll option. Player A passes to B and moves to set a screen for B. As B dribbles the defense switches to cover her. A rolls to the basket for a return pass from B.

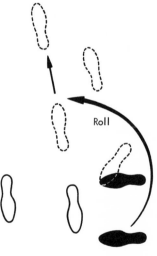

Roll

Figure 5.8 Footwork of the roll.

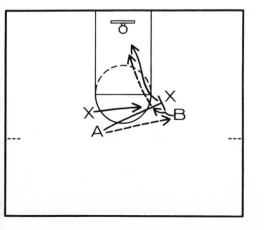

The *screen and roll* may also be executed from the forward-to-rover position with a slight variation in the position of the screen. This variation can be seen in Fig. 5.10.

DRIBBLE PATTERN

The player with the ball may decide to dribble rather than pass to initiate a two-player pattern. She may decide to dribble to the outside of a stationary teammate and try to force her defensive player into this stationary screen, freeing herself for a continued drive to the basket or a jump shot option.

Another option is to dribble to an inside screen position and hand the ball off to a teammate as she cuts close by the dribbler's side for a drive to the basket. This pattern is sometimes called a weave; if the drive is not available, it can be continued until the drive or shot is achieved. The screener should roll toward the basket. This pattern may involve two, three, or all four players.

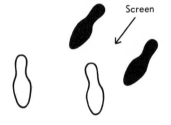

Figure 5.10 Foot position—a forward screens for a rover.

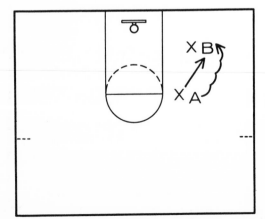

Figure 5.11 Dribble rub. Player A dribbles close to B and forces her defensive player out of position. A is freed for a possible shot or drive.

PASS AND SCREEN AWAY

A player may decide to pass the ball to one teammate and set a screen for another player away from the ball. Usually, a screen away from the ball is not as effective as one on the ball. Figure 5.13 is an example of a possible screening pattern away from the ball. This will involve three offensive players.

POST PATTERNS

There are several types of play patterns that involve a post player. The post player is identified by the position she assumes on the playing court. Normally, she is a tall player who stations

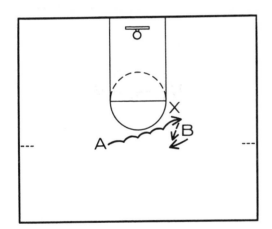

Figure 5.12 Dribble weave. Player A dribbles inside B and hands the ball off, thus setting a screen for B.

Figure 5.13 Pass and screen away from the ball. Player A passes to B and moves to set a screen for C. B passes to C as she cuts toward the basket.

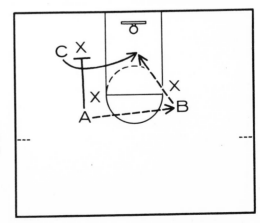

herself somewhere close to the free throw lane and plays part of the time with her back to the basket. She is referred to as a low post when playing within a few feet of the basket, and a high post when playing near the free throw line.

Some of the patterns already described may be worked with a post player; for example, a pass into the post and cut as shown in Fig. 5.15 and a dribble rub-off the post player as shown in Fig. 5.16 indicate how their plays can be made.

One of the most common post plays is a pattern called *splitting the post*. The post player will station herself between the two rovers or between a rover and forward. In a rover—and—post situation, the play is initiated by either rover with a pass into the post player. The passer fakes in one direction, moves in the opposite one, and becomes the first

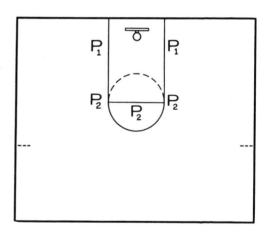

Figure 5.14 Possible post positions. P1 is at the low post positions; P2 is at the high post positions.

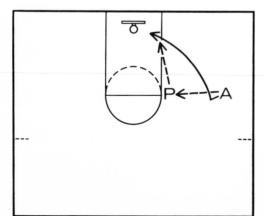

Figure 5.15 Pass to post and cut. Player A passes to P and cuts. She receives a return pass from P.

cutter as she breaks close to the post player on her way to the basket. As the first cutter passes the post player the second rover fakes in one direction and then cuts to the opposite side of the post player. The post player may either hand off or pass the ball to the first or second cutter. She also has the options of shooting or driving with the ball herself.

There are numerous variations on a pattern with a post player using two- and three-player combinations. One variation of a splitting-the-post pattern can be made by using a screen away from the ball. The pattern begins with the pass to the post player, but instead of a cut to the basket the player moves to set a screen for the second cutter and then continues her cut to the basket. The post player has the same options as before.

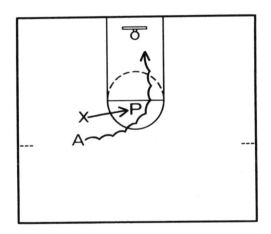

Figure 5.16 Dribble rub with post. Player A dribbles close to the post, forcing her defensive player out of position.

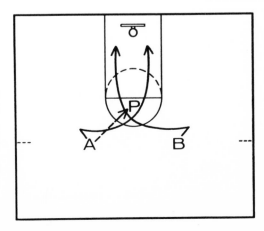

Figure 5.17 Splitting the post. Player A passes to P and cuts close to the far side of P. P may hand the ball off to A or B, pass later to A or B, or turn and take a shot herself.

DEFENSIVE COMBINATIONS

In basketball, as in other sports, for every offensive move there is a defensive countermove. There are numerous defensive tactics for two players that, when used effectively, will counter the offensive patterns. The following are some general rules for basic defense:

1. The defensive player stays between her opponent and the basket or between her opponent and the ball when in close range of the basket.

2. When the opponent passes the ball, the defensive player must sink quickly in the direction of the pass, look for screens, and block off the opponents possible cutting lanes.

3. The defensive players must talk to each other to coordinate the timing necessary for the defensive adjustments and to alert each other to screens, switches, and other maneuvers.

Generally, one of three different approaches is followed to counter the screens used in basketball. The preferred defensive adjustment is for the defensive player to continue to guard her offensive player by moving in front of the screen set to prevent her movement. A properly executed screen will prevent this adjustment.

The second method against a screen is the maneuver of sliding behind or around the screen and continuing to guard the same offensive player. As the two offensive players come

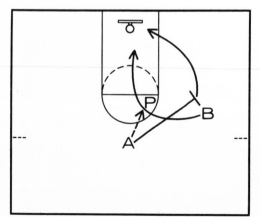

Figure 5.18 Splitting the post—variation. Player A passes to P and moves to screen for B. B cuts by P, and A continues her move to the basket.

together forming the screen situation it is sometimes necessary for the defensive player's teammates to take a step backward to allow her to slide through one player removed from the ball. The apparent weakness of this adjustment is that it would give the offensive player time to stop and shoot while the defensive player is going behind the screen, but this is only a concern to the defensive player when the offensive player is within her shooting range.

When the shot behind the screen is apparent, or the defensive player is unable to get past the screen, a third type of adjustment is used. In this situation the defensive players exchange assignments. The defensive player who was originally responsible for the screener picks up the player freed by the screen. Several methods are possible to accomplish this "switch." The following is one of the simpler methods. As the defensive player responsible for the screener becomes aware of the screener's intent, she begins to verbally warn her teammate of the screen. For example, she might call "screen right" as the screen moves to her teammate's right. Just as the screen is set, the defensive player being screened adjusts by quickly moving back about a foot as her teammate moves to a position along her side about an elbow's distance apart. This position of the defensive players will prevent the screener from rolling. The player with the ball is picked up by whichever defensive player she moves toward from the midline position between the two defensive players. If the "switch" is necessary, it is called verbally to help avoid confusion. The "switch" call does not literally mean that a switch is made at that time, but that one will automatically be made if it is necessary to do so.

Figure 5.19 Moving over the top of a screen.

Figure 5.20 Sliding through. The player at the far left has dropped back, allowing her teammate to continue guarding Number 10.

Figure 5.21   Defensive switch.

Defending the post player and possible post screens requires special considerations. When the post player is in a low post position, every effort should be made to prevent her from receiving the pass. The defensive player should play to the ball side of the post player with a hand in the passing lane.

When the post player is close to the basket and a pass to her is possible, the defensive player may be forced to move between the post player and the basket. This is with the assumption that the players are about the same height.

If the post player moves to a high post position, the job becomes easier. In this case the defensive player stays between the post player and the basket, but is still pressuring on the ball side. When the high post receives the ball, the defensive player must drop off and assume a normal defensive position for a player with the dribble option.

The following is a reaction to the single cutter off the post. As the pass is made into the post the player defending the passer sinks off quickly in the direction of the pass and feels with her back hand for the post screen. The player pressing the post player backs off quickly as the pass is received. This provides room for her to properly defend the post player while giving her teammate room to slide through if necessary.

Figure 5.22 Defensive position when the high post receives the ball.

Team
Defense

There are two different types of team defense: the *player-to-player* and the *zone*. In the player-to-player defensive system, the primary responsibility of each defensive player is to her assigned opponent. The defensive player will stay with her assigned player wherever she moves around the defensive court. With a zone defensive system, the responsibility of each defensive player is to her assigned area of the court. Therefore, the defensive player in a zone will assume the responsibility for any player coming into her area of the court. Sometimes a combination of a zone and player-to-player defense will be used. Both types of defense require the ability to execute the individual defensive techniques.

Both systems have advantages and disadvantages; for this reason, some teams will prefer to use both. The player-to-player defense is a more versatile type than the zone defense because it permits a defensive effort in any area of the playing court, whereas the zone is limited to an area primarily around the lane. Often a player will find the player-to-player defense more of a personal challenge because she consistently matches her abilities against a particular opponent. An advantage of the zone is that it is rather easy to learn; however, it tends to weaken the individual defensive fundamentals. These are but a few of the advantages and disadvantages of the different types of team defenses.

PLAYER-TO-PLAYER DEFENSE

The player-to-player defensive system has several variations. The straight, switching, sagging, and pressing player-to-player defenses are examples. The type used would depend upon the objectives of the defense and upon the abilities of the offense.

The following is a set of rules for an assigned player-to-player defense. The assignments are made matching speed, size, and ability of players as much as possible. Usually it is advisable to have rovers responsible for rovers, and guards responsible for guards.

1. **Challenge the ball.** The player with the ball must be actively defended when she comes within a few feet of her own shooting range. Obviously, this distance will differ with each player. If the shooting range of the opponents is not known, the rule may be to pick up any offensive player with the ball when she enters a certain area of the court. The area inside the top of the circle extended to the baseline (see Fig. 6.1) will sufficiently cover the normal shooting range of the average woman player.

2. **Point the ball.** As the ball is passed the defensive player slides back off the player or sags in the direction of the pass. She tries to point at the ball with one hand and at her player with the other hand. This allows her to see the total offensive and defensive actions. One of the common mistakes of the beginning player is to follow the offensive player around the court without considering her relationship to the total team effort.

3. **Switch.** A switch is used only when absolutely necessary and within the court area described in rule one.

4. **Help on defense.** When an offensive player is able to drive or evades her defensive player, she then becomes the responsibility of the defensive player closest to her. All players on defense should be prepared to "help out" or "call for help" when necessary.

5. **Force the offense inside.** The defensive player should protect the baseline drive with good defensive position and force the drive to the middle of the court where help from teammates is available.

6. **Talk on defense.** The four defensive players should continually talk and warn each other of "screens," "switches," "help," and "clears" (areas where no help is available).

7. **Block out and rebound.** When the shot goes up, turn and block your opponent out, then get the rebound. This prevents the second shot by the offense.

ZONE DEFENSE

Three popular zone combinations are used with the four-player defense of women's basketball. They are the 2–2, or box zone; the 1–2–1, or diamond zone; and the 1–1–2 zone. These combinations determine how the court is divided into individual defensive areas of responsibility. The box and diamond zones are the most commonly used formations.

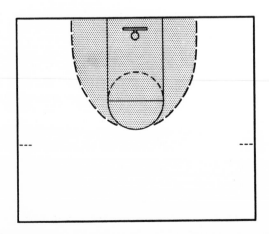

Figure 6.1 Defensive area—top of the circle extended.

Figure 6.2   Zone defenses.

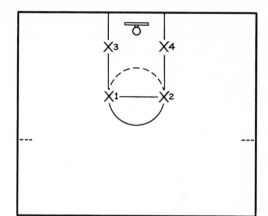

A. 2—2 zone.

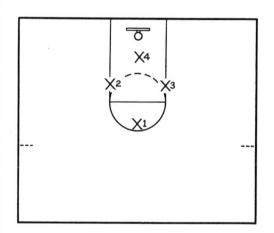

B. 1—2—1 zone.

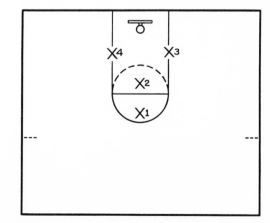

C. 1—1—2 zone.

Basically, the idea of a zone is to keep the same relative formation while it is continually adjusting and shifting to the movement and position of the ball. This formation will vary with the objectives of the defense and abilities of the offense.

Each zone has its own particular strengths and weaknesses. It is generally felt that the greatest weakness of the box zone is the middle. The baseline area on both sides of the basket tend to be the weakest area of the diamond zone.

The following is a general set of rules for a zone defense:

1. **Establish zone quickly.** Players must change from offense to defense and set the zone up quickly. Often in beginning basketball the guards will play the back spaces of a zone, and the rovers will play the spaces closest to the center line.

Figure 6.3 Basic 2—2 shifts.

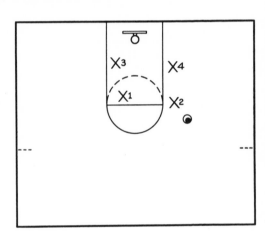

A. Shift of 2—2 zone with the ball at a rover position.

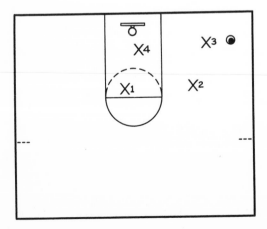

B. Shift of 2—2 zone with the ball in the corner.

2. **All defensive players face the ball.** The players in the zone watch and shift quickly to each movement of the ball.

3. **Protect the zone.** When an offensive player enters an area of the zone and is a possible pass receiver, the player responsible for that area must assume player-to-player responsibilities for her until she has left the area.

4. **Hands up.** The players should keep their hands up, increasing the size and pass-deflecting abilities of the zone. However, to improve the speed and ease of the move, it is advisable for the players to lower their hands as the shift is made and then to raise them again quickly.

Figure 6.3 shows the basic 2−2 shifts with the movement of the ball, and Fig. 6.4 shows the basic 1−2−1 shifts with the ball as it moves around the zone.

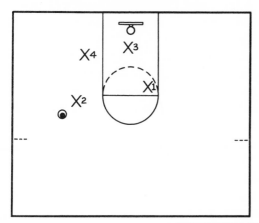

Figure 6.4 Basic 1−2−1 shifts.

A. Shift of 1−2−1 zone with the ball at a rover position.

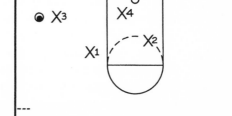

B. Shift of 1−2−1 zone with the ball in the corner.

Team
Offense

In the game of women's basketball any four players may combine at one time on one half of the court to form the team's offense. There are two basic styles of offensive team play. One is the running, free-lance type of play, and the other is the control game with deliberate play patterns. Some teams use a combination of styles where they attempt to run with the ball or fast break, hoping to gain an advantage over the defense for an easy shot. If this fails, they set up and go into some type of control play.

With a team offense, regardless of the style of play, *floor balance* and continuity of movement must be considered. To establish floor balance, each player must know her position and be aware of her responsibilities on the court; at the same time she must also be familiar with her teammates' positions. This balance will vary with the basic type of offensive pattern used. A common offensive mistake is for the players to continually crowd the middle of the court or for all to move toward the ball; when they do this they eliminate possible cutting lanes and offensive rebounding positions. Another mistake occurs when one team member is unaware of what her teammates are trying to work and she actually gets in their way. Therefore, to coordinate the movements of four players into a team effort some simple rules must be followed. The following are offered as some general guides. To begin with, a player must understand the floor balance and the responsibilities of her position and that of her teammates. To coordinate the action, the rover with the ball will initiate, or "key," the play patterns. When a player is not directly involved with the play pattern, she should try to occupy her defensive player and at the same time stay out of the way of her teammates. Finally, there must be a continuity of movement of "keeping the ball moving" to gain an advantage over the defense. Slow player and ball movement allow the defense time to recover and adjust their efforts.

There are numerous types of basic play patterns. Four of the more commonly used will be discussed in this chapter. The types of offense the team decides upon will depend upon the size and ability of the players involved. The type or types chosen should be those that will best utilize the total team potential. The variation of the type or types used in the game will be determined by the defense used by the opponent, all other things being equal.

FOUR-OUT OFFENSE

The four-out offense is one of the most commonly used types of team offense in women's basketball. It is employed most often by a team with balanced height and ability that does not have a good tall player. Figure 7.1 shows the basic offensive pattern, A and B are rovers, C and D are forwards. From this position the two-player patterns discussed in Chapter 5 can be utilized with the addition of the general rules of a team offense. The number and complexity of combinations possible are almost limitless. The key to an effective offense is a simple combination well learned and properly executed. A simple play pattern run from the four-out offense is shown in Fig. 7.2.

Player A passes to B and cuts. If A does not receive the pass, she sets a screen for D, who moves across the lane for a possible pass. Again, if there is no pass, then D moves to the position held by C, and C balances out to the vacant spot left by A. Player B is then free to pass to D, and the whole movement is repeated with B cutting first. This is a simple version of a shuffle offense. A shuffle offense is a continuity pattern that eliminates one of the disadvantages of set plays. A set play must be reset after each attempt if it fails to result in a score. In the shuffle offense, after all the options have been run, the plays are set up ready to run the pattern again. All players must learn to play all positions, although variations can be developed to change this; for example, by keeping a tall player close to the basket.

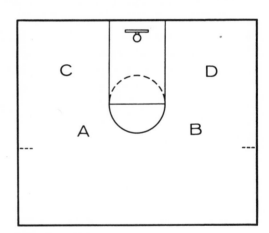

Figure 7.1 Basic four-out offensive formation.

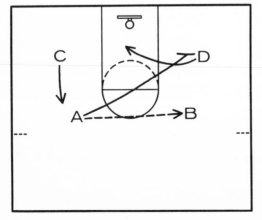

Figure 7.2 A four-out play pattern.

SINGLE-POST OFFENSE

The *single-post offense* is probably the most common offensive pattern known to basketball. It utilizes the abilities of a tall player with three shorter teammates. Figure 7.3 shows the basic position of the single post. A and B are in the rover position, D is in a forward position, and C is in a high post position. The post player is free to move to any side of the lane, in either a high or low post position. The post player has a potential reverse shot when she receives the ball in a low post position. Figure 7.4 shows one method for getting the ball to the low post player. Player B passes to D, fakes a move toward A, and cuts down the middle. If open, B will receive the ball for a shot. If not open, B continues on through the lane and sets a screen for C, the low post. This can be used most effectively

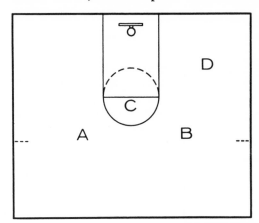

Figure 7.3 Basic single-post formation.

Figure 7.4 Single-post play. Player B passes to D and cuts down the middle. If B does not receive the ball, she screens for C who cuts across the lane for a pass.

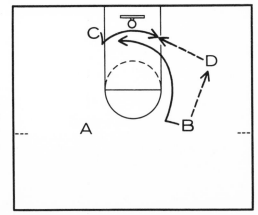

against a switching player-to-player defense. It can force a switch of defensive responsibilities resulting in a shorter player guarding the low post.

There are many variations of a *splitting the post* pattern. Figure 7.5 is one variation of the split from a high post position. A passes to C; as the pass is made D cuts toward the baseline. A sets a screen for D. If B does not receive the pass, C tries to pass to D coming off the screen set by A.

DOUBLE-POST OFFENSE

The *double-post offense* is used when a team has two tall players it would like to keep close to the basket, and two smaller players who can handle the ball and shoot from outside.

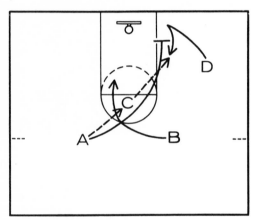

Figure 7.5 Variation of splitting the post. Player A passes to C, D cuts toward baseline. Players A and B split the post. If B is not free, C passes to D moving off screen set by A.

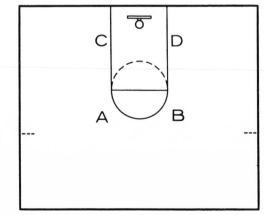

Figure 7.6 Basic double-post formation.

Figure 7.6 shows the basic floor positions. A and B are the rovers, and C and D are the post players. A play using the double-post formation is shown in Fig. 7.7. Player B passes to A and cuts to the other side of the lane moving in front of D and sets a screen for C. Player D cuts toward the ball and receives a pass from A; A then cuts outside D. Player D may pass to A, drive the middle of the lane, or pass to C cutting off the screen set by B.

TANDEM POST OFFENSE

The *tandem post offense* is another type of pattern using two post players. Figure 7.8 shows the basic formation. A is referred to as the "point player" and directs the play, B is the

Figure 7.7 A double-post play. Player B passes to A and cuts across the lane in front of D. D cuts toward the ball and receives a pass from A. A then cuts outside of D. D may pass to A, drive lane, or pass to C, cutting off the screen set by B.

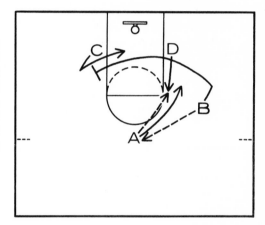

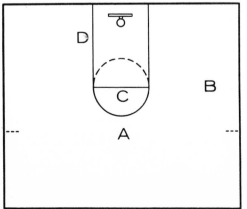

Figure 7.8 Basic tandem post formation.

"wing player," C is the high post, and D is the low post. This pattern can be set up on either side of the floor and will work against both the player-to-player and the zone defenses.

The following are several variations of a pattern off a pass from the point-to-wing position. In Fig. 7.9 player A passes to B, fakes left, and rubs her defensive player off on the high post. B passes to A for a shot. If A is not open for a pass, C may cut off of A who has formed a moving screen for C, freeing her for a pass and shot. There is still another vatiation of this play: If A is covered, she will cut across the lane and set a screen for the low post D who cuts across the lane for a pass from B.

The first rule of offense is to determine what defense is being employed and to play accordingly. Remember that against a player-to-player defense the offensive player will be taking a defensive player with her as she moves around the court. The screen-and-roll, give-and-go, and weave maneuvers work best against a player-to-player defense. Fast passes, good outside shooting, screens, and overloading an area of the court work best against a zone defense.

FAST BREAK

The fast break is a method of beating the defense down the court with the ball to gain the advantage for an easy shot or layup. In women's basketball this will most often develop into a situation with three offensive players against two offensive players or a three-on-two situation.

Since the success of the fast break depends upon how quickly the ball can be moved down the court, the ball must be moved at a fast pace. This results in more ball-handling errors than would normally occur. For this reason many people consider the fast break an advanced technique; when run successfully, it is one of the most enjoyable play patterns of the game.

The fast break can be initiated whenever the ball is turned over to the opposing team. It is most easily initiated from an

Figure 7.9   Tandem post play.

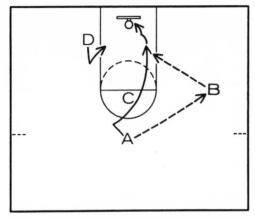

A. Player A passes to B and rubs her defensive player off on C. B passes to A for a shot.

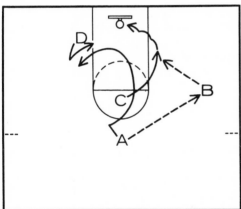

B. If A is covered as she breaks by C, C cuts behind A for a pass from B.

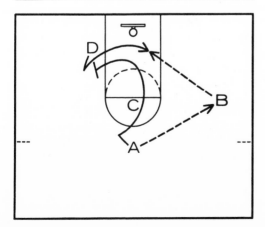

C. (Variation of 7.9A) If A does not receive the pass, she moves on through the lane and sets a screen for D who cuts to receive a pass from B.

interception in the back court or from a ʳebound. Figure 7.10 shows a fast-break pattern from a rebound. Player A rebounds the ball and executes a quick pass, commonly called the "outlet pass," to rover C. C passes to rover D who has run to the middle of the court. D then dribbles, staying in the middle of the court, toward the basket ahead of the defense. If player D is challenged by the defense, she passes to her free teammate, player F, cutting toward the basket. There are many other types of formations for fast-break developments.

Figure 7.10   Possible fast-break pattern.

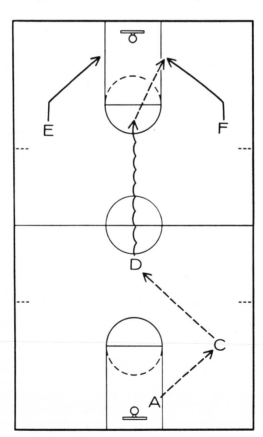

Special
Game
Situations

The individual and team procedures discussed in the preceding chapters are combined with situations and strategies developed and controlled within a set of rules. These rules have prescribed the framework for the development of basketball skills and strategies; but just because of the development of these skills and strategies there is a continual need to re-examine and change the rules. Thus the evolution of basketball continues from its simple 13 rule origin to the fast, challenging, and exciting game of today. The following are some situations and strategies used in the present game.

JUMP-BALL

The team formation during a jump ball depends upon the restraining circle in which it is taken and the possible outcome of the jump. When a team thinks it can control the ball, the jumper tries to tap the ball either to a space between two of her teammates or to a teammate's open side away from the defense. When a team thinks it cannot control the

63

jump ball, the players must be alert to read the situation and possibly intercept the tap, but the first consideration is proper defense to prevent a shot.

During a *jump ball at the center circle* one guard should remain back around the top of the circle for defense. The other players on the team establish positions around the circle. The exact positions around the circle depend upon the probable results of the tap. Figure 8.3 shows the positions used when the result of the tap is uncertain.

When the jump ball is taken at a restraining circle near a basket, the team formation is determined by which team's front court it is in and by the possible result of the tap. When a team

Figure 8.1 Jump ball.

Figure 8.2 Jump ball game situation notice how Number 22 (black shirt) has read the play and stepped in front of her opponent.

expects to control the tap in its front court, an offensive position, as shown in Fig. 8.4, is used. When the control of the tap is uncertain, or improbable, the team might use a defensive alignment as shown in Fig. 8.5.

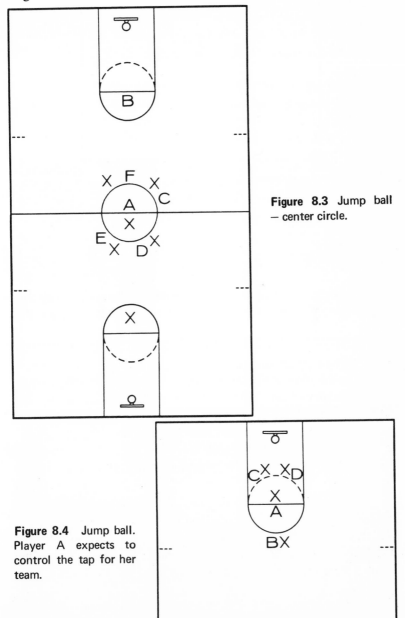

Figure 8.3 Jump ball — center circle.

Figure 8.4 Jump ball. Player A expects to control the tap for her team.

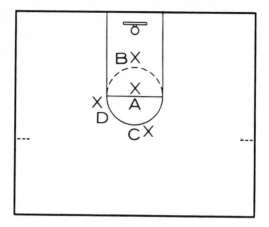

Figure 8.5 Jump ball. Player A believes her opponent will control the tap.

FREE THROW

The rules of basketball determine the possible strategy that can be used to best advantage during the free throw. According to the rules, the team's members must line up at the free throw lane in alternating spaces. At least one player from each team must take a space on each side of the basket. The offensive team has the choice of side for the space closest to the basket. The defensive team gets the corresponding space on the opposite side of the lane. All players must remain outside the lane until the ball has touched the rim or entered the basket.

Strategically, the offensive team will place their tallest and most skilled shooter on her preferred shooting side of the basket.

The defensive team will place its tallest and most skilled rebounders in its two spaces closest to the basket. The defensive player in the third space out from the basket is responsible for blocking out the shooter. The remaining player, depending upon the defensive rebounding strength of the team, may rebound along the lane or position herself for a possible outlet pass and start of a fast break.

As a general rule, the defensive rebounders should play for possession of the ball. The offensive rebounders may choose to tip the ball to a teammate or back into the basket, rather than play for individual possession. One of the common mistakes of a beginning player is to jump from behind the lane line to obtain the rebound rather than to move into a more advantageous position before jumping.

OUT-OF-BOUNDS

According to the rules, after a free throw or field goal the ball is put into play by an opponent from behind the baseline. Strategically, a guard should obtain the ball as quickly as possible and throw it in-bounds from the side of the basket that corresponds to her preferred throwing hand. Generally, as the guard takes the ball out-of-bounds the rovers will move to opposite sides of the court and the remaining guard will take a position in the middle of the court as is shown in Fig. 8.7.

The ball is also put into play from out-of-bounds along the sidelines and endlines after violations. Usually the closest guard will put the ball back into play from the sidelines of her back court. This frees the rovers to move down court more quickly.

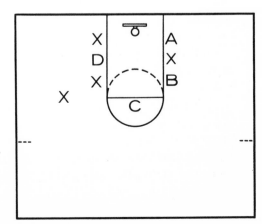

Figure 8.6   Free-throw situation.

In more advanced basketball, set plays may be run from the sideline or endline. Figure 8.8 shows a possible endline play from a team's front court.

GENERAL TEAM STRATEGY

The first consideration of a team's strategy is to determine the type of offense and defense being used by the opponents and adjust accordingly. Usually it is wise to dictate the first offensive move of the game to read the defense. For example, if a rover cuts through the middle of the lane to the baseline, and one person follows her, it is a player-to-player defense.

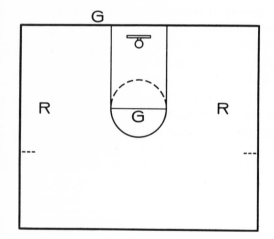

Figure 8.7   Endline throw-in after score.

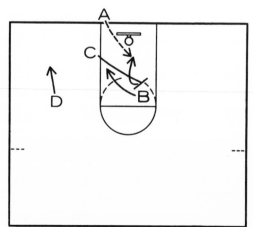

Figure 8.8 Endline out-of-bounds play. Player C sets screen for B. As B cuts off C's screen C rolls toward the basket. If defense switches to cover B, C should be open for a pass.

Rules of Basketball

Basketball rules in the United States are established by a joint committee of the Division for Girls' and Women's Sports and the Amateur Athletic Union. Two separate guides, which include identical rules, are published yearly by these organization. The following is a synopsis of the DGWS-AAU official basketball rules for girls and women, sufficient for playing a game.

PLAYING COURT

There are several areas and markings of the court with which a player must be familiar. (See Fig. 9.1.)

PLAYERS AND SUBSTITUTES

Each team consists of six players, plus any number of substitutes. Any four players on a team may be in one half of the court at one time. This means that two players from each team may play the entire court.

A substitute may enter the game any number of times. She must report her name and number to the scorer and may enter the game at the first dead ball, after being beckoned into the game by the official.

Between quarters and halves a substitute may enter the game after reporting to the scorer.

SCORING AND TIMING

Two points are awarded for a *field goal*. A field goal is scored when the ball legally enters the basket during normal play. *One point* is scored for a *free throw*. A free throw is an unguarded shot at the basket. It is awarded as the result of certain infractions of the rules by an opponent. The team with the most points at the end of the playing time is declared the winner.

Figure 9.1 Basketball court.

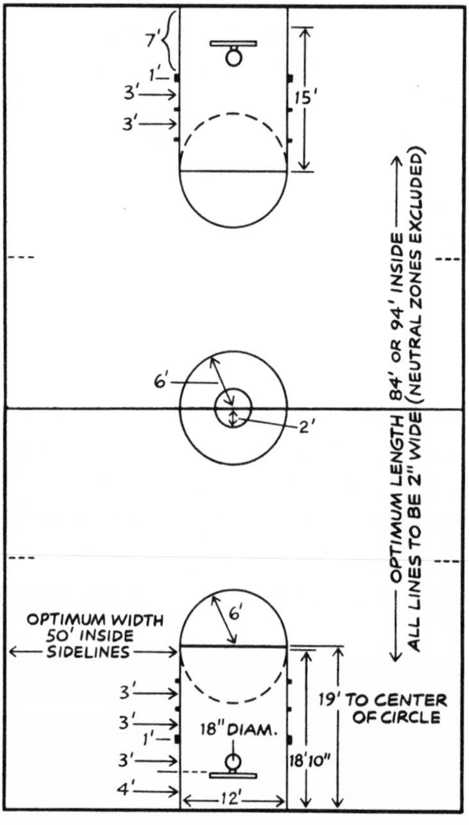

The game consists of 4 eight-minute quarters of actual playing time. There is a two-minute intermission between each quarter and a ten-minute intermission between halves. If the score is tied at the end of the regulation playing time, 1 or more three-minute overtime periods are played. There is a two-minute intermission between overtime periods. Each team is allowed 5 time-outs during regulation play. An additional time-out is awarded for each overtime period. Each quarter is started with a jump ball between any two opposing players at the center restraining circle. The playing time continues until a foul, jump ball, or time-out for rest or substitution occurs.

PLAYING THE BALL

The *jump ball* is a method of putting the ball into play. The official tosses the ball upward between the two opposing jumpers. The jumpers must stay in their own half of the restraining circle and face their respective baskets. All other players must remain outside the restraining circle until after the ball is tapped. The jumpers may tap the ball twice in succession, but neither may touch the ball again until it has touched the floor or another player.

After each field goal or successful free throw the ball is put into play by a throw-in from out of bounds at the opponents' baseline.

There are certain ways in which a player may legally handle the ball: She may throw, roll, bounce, hand, or tap it to another player. She may catch, shoot, or throw the ball with one or both hands. She may advance the ball herself by means of a dribble. The initial impetus for the dribble may be given with two hands, but continued impetus may be given by only one hand at a time, and any number of steps may be taken between each bounce of the ball. A player has 5 seconds to attempt a throw-in from out of bounds and 10 seconds to attempt a free throw. She may hold the ball for 5 seconds when closely guarded. She may tap the ball from an opponent's hands, or tie the ball by firmly placing her hand on the ball already held by an opponent. She has to stop within two steps at the completion of a dribble or pass caught on the run.

VIOLATIONS AND PENALTIES

A violation is an infringement of a rule. After the violation the ball is awarded to the opponents out-of-bounds at the sideline opposite the spot where the violation occurred. The ball is taken out-of-bounds at the engline when the ball or player with the ball goes over the endline. It is a violation to:

1. Leave one's own half of the restraining circle or tap the ball more than twice on a jump ball.
2. Enter the restraining circle before the ball is tapped by one of the jumpers.
3. Kick or strike the ball.
4. Dribble again after the first dribble is completed.
5. Hold the ball for more than 5 seconds when closely guarded, more than 5 seconds out-of-bounds, or more than 10 seconds on a free throw.
6. Cause the ball to go out-of-bounds.
7. Remain for more than 3 seconds in the free throw lane without the ball when the player's team has possession of the ball in its front court.
8. Have a fifth player from one team on one half of the court. (No violation is called if it would be a disadvantage to the opponents.)
9. Walk or run with the ball.
10. Step over the line before the ball touches the ring or enters the basket during a free throw.
11. Fail to make the ball touch the ring or enter the basket when attempting a free throw.

FOULS AND PENALTIES

A foul is an infraction of the rules. Personal contact, which can often result in roughness, is considered a foul and is charged to the player who causes the contact. The penalty is the awarding of 1 or more free throws, depending upon the situation in which the foul occurs. A player is awarded 1 free throw when she is fouled against, unless she is in the act of shooting. If the shooter makes the basket, she is awarded 1 free throw. If she misses the basket, 2 free throws are awarded. In the *last two minutes* of play 2 free throws are awarded for each one-foul situation. When two players foul simultaneously (double foul), each player is given a foul and awarded 1 free throw. The game is resumed with a center jump ball between any two opponents. It is a foul to:

1. **block** Impede the progress of an opponent by means of personal contact. Two forms of blocking are: (1) entering the established path of an opponent without giving her a chance to stop or change direction, and (2) interfering with the progress of an opponent by holding the arms fully extended horizontally.
2. **charge** A player with the ball contacts an opponent whose position or path is legally established.
3. **tag** Contact an opponent repeatedly with hand, elbow, or body.
4. **push.**
5. **hold.**
6. **trip.**
7. Use **unnecessary roughness** which might cause injury to an opponent.
8. **threaten the eyes** Use hands in a dangerous manner toward the eyes of a player with the ball.
9. Use **unsportsmanlike conduct.**
10. **Disconcert** the shooter or **interfere** with the ball during a free throw.

TEAM FOULS AND DISQUALIFICATIONS

For certain infractions of the rules a foul is given to the team. For each team foul the opponents are awarded a free throw. Any player may attempt a free throw. It is a team foul to:

1. substitute illegally
2. leave the court without permission
3. fail to raise one's hand after committing a foul
4. take more than 5 team time-outs

Any player receiving as many as 5 fouls—or one disqualifying foul—is removed from the game and not permitted to re-enter.

Game
Evaluation

The techniques discussed in this chapter are primarily concerned with evaluating and understanding the team effort of basketball. The individual skill evaluations are viewed in terms of their contributing strengths and weaknesses to the team effort. This is not intended as an individual skills test.

CHARTING BASKETBALL

The information available from the official score book and from observations of individual persons provide a limited view of what actually occurred during the game. The purpose of charting the game is to obtain objective data that will provide a more complete view of the game. This information is used as a comprehensive guide for future individual and team development.

A few of the most commonly used types of charting techniques involve shooting, rebounding, ball control errors, and the jump balls. In some cases all of these will be charted, whereas in others only a few will be charted. The choices are based upon the individual needs of the team. The team should have a definite purpose in mind for the use of the information, which should be noted as concisely as possible so that it will be of value.

Of the various charting techniques mentioned, the shot chart is the one most frequently used. It is kept while the game is being played and provides the following information: number of shots taken, type of shots taken, location of shots taken, and shooting percentages of the individuals and team. This chart takes the form of a diagram of a basketball court as shown in Fig. 10.1, which also illustrates the charting technique. When a shot is attempted it is recorded by writing the number of the player attempting the shot at the approximate place on the court where the shot was taken. If the basket is made, the number is circled. The type of shot may be identified by placing a symbol beside the number. A different colored marking is used to separate the shots taken by quarters. The shot chart can be broken down into an individual shot chart after the game is over.

Figure 10.1   Shot chart.

Date_____   SFVSC vs. _____   Location_____

No.	Name	SA	SM	%	FTA	FTM	%	Off. Reb.	Def. Reb.	Assist	Steal	Block	Turn-over	Jump Ball Tap	Jump Ball Reb.	Fouls
31	SMITH	20	10	50	8	4	50	6	0	3	1	0	1	W-1 L-1	2	2
	TEAM TOTALS															

Much useful information might be drawn from the shot chart. For example, the number of shots taken can point to specific weaknesses and strengths of the individual or team in offensive and defensive play. If too few shots were taken, it might be wise to practice more on offense. The chart will show who is shooting most often; it will also indicate whom to guard more closely during the game. The types of shots taken may help to determine the kind of shooting practice needed or what type of defensive adjustment to make. In addition, the location of the shot will indicate an area for offensive improvement or defensive adjustment. If the opposing team is shooting a number of outside shots unsuccessfully, a sagging type of player-to-player or a zone defense might be effective. The shooting percentage can be used in a positive manner to motivate the team into working for better shots.

Another important consideration in team evaluation and eventual improvement is knowing who is getting the ball, who is losing it, and how this is happening. Figure 10.2 is an example of a chart that will help answer some of these questions. When keeping this chart, the number of the player who executes the particular action is written in the corresponding column. Looking at the mistakes committed can be a guide in helping plan the practice program. Figure 10.3 shows a composite charting picture. However, there are nearly as many types and combinations of charts as there are different teams. Many people prefer to use one paper, which combines shot charts, the incidents chart, and whatever else they have chosen to record.

Whatever charting techniques you finally select, remember to study the charts carefully after each game; use them in a constructive and positive manner to help improve the individual or team effort. Interpret the statistics in the light of the type of offense or defense used and the skill level of the team. Only through charting will you become aware of the specific needs of your team—its weaknesses and strengths—and by applying your knowledge to the best of your ability, you will play a vital part in the future success of your team.

Figure 10.2 Incident chart.

Date _____	SFVSC vs. _____

REBOUNDS

Offensive	Defensive
31 32 31 31	

Assists	Steals	Blocks
26 32		

TURNOVERS

Bad pass	Traveling
	31
Illegal dribble	
Line violation	Fumble
22	
Held ball	
	Taken away
3 sec.	

Possession	JUMP BALL	Control tap
22	Won 31 31	
	Lost	

Figure 10.3 Composite chart. SA = Shots Attempted; SM = Shots Made; FTA = Free Throws Attempted; FTM = Free Throws Made.

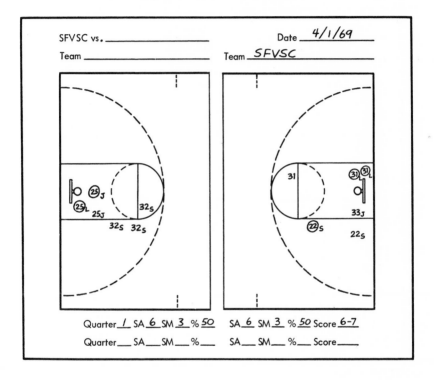

Suggested Readings

Brown, Lyle, *Offensive and Defensive Drills for Winning Basketball*. Englewood Cliffs, New Jersey: Prentice-Hall Inc., 1965.

Gardner, Jack, *Championship Basketball with Jack Gardner*. Englewood Cliffs, N.J.: Prentice-Hall Inc., 1963.

McLane, Hardin, *Championship Basketball by 12 Great Coaches*. Englewood Cliffs, N.J.: Prentice-Hall Inc., 1965.

Newell, Pete, and John Bennington, *Basketball Methods*. New York, N.Y.: The Ronald Press Company, 1962.

Weyand, Alexander M., *The Cavalcade of Basketball*. New York, N.Y.: The Macmillan Company, 1960.

Wilkes, Glenn, *Winning Basketball Strategy*. Englewood Cliffs, N.J.: Prentice-Hall Inc., 1959.

Wooden, John R., *Practical Modern Basketball*. New York, N.Y.: The Ronald Press Company, 1966.